HOW It's MADE

A Glass Jar

Sarah Ridley

GARETH**STEVENS**
PUBLISHING
A Member of the WRC Media Family of Companies

Please visit our web site at: www.garethstevens.com
For a free color catalog describing Gareth Stevens Publishing's list of high-quality books
and multimedia programs, call 1-800-542-2595 (USA) or 1-800-387-3178 (Canada).
Gareth Stevens Publishing's fax: (414) 332-3567.

Library of Congress Cataloging-in-Publication Data

Ridley, Sarah, 1963-
  A glass jar / Sarah Ridley.
      p. cm. – (How it's made)
  ISBN-10: 0-8368-6701-7 – ISBN-13: 978-0-8368-6701-5 (lib. bdg.)
  1. Glass containers–Juvenile literature.   2. Glass manufacture–Juvenile literature.   I. Title.   II. Series.
  TP865.R53   2006
  666`.192–dc22
                                                                    2006042293

This North American edition first published in 2007 by
Gareth Stevens Publishing
A Member of the WRC Media Family of Companies
330 West Olive Street, Suite 100
Milwaukee, WI 53212 USA

This U.S. edition copyright © 2007 by Gareth Stevens, Inc.
Original edition copyright © 2006 by Franklin Watts.
First published in Great Britain in 2006 by Franklin Watts,
338 Euston Road, London NW1 3BH, United Kingdom.

Series editor: Sarah Peutrill
Art director: Jonathan Hair
Designer: Jemima Lumley

Gareth Stevens editor: Tea Benduhn
Gareth Stevens art direction: Tammy West
Gareth Stevens graphic designer: Charlie Dahl

Photo credits: (t=top, b=bottom, l=left, r=right, c=center)
James L. Amos/CORBIS: 22, 27tl. Ancient Art & Architecture Collection/Topfoto: 9b. Arco/La Terra Magica/Alamy: 16,
26cr. Yann Arthus-Bertrand/CORBIS: 7t. Justin Case/Alamy: 30bl. CORBIS: 25b. Bob Daemmrich/Image Works/Topfoto:
5t. Digital Vision: 6b, 11t, 15b, 26cl. DK Limited/CORBIS: 8, 26tl. Mark E. Gibson/CORBIS: 10t. Jeff Greenberg/Image
Works/Topfoto: 13b. Reino Hanninen/Alamy: 6t. Holt Confer/Image Works/Topfoto: 15c. Andre Jenny/Alamy: 31b. Mary
Evans Picture Library: 19b. Sandi McDonald/Alamy: 31t. Ray Moller/Watts: front cover br, 1, 4, 5b, 23br, 27br. Kevin R.
Morris/Bohemian Nomad Picturemakers/CORBIS: 10b. Pilkington plc: 17bl, 17br. Rockware Glass Ltd.: front cover c, back
cover both, 9t, 11b, 12 both, 13t, 14 both, 15t, 20, 21t, 24, 25t, 26bl, 26tr, 27c, 27tr. Heini Schneebeli/SPL: 17t, 26br. Science &
Society Picture Library: 21b. Sygma/CORBIS: 23bl. Watts: 3, 28-29, 30br. Whitestone Diomedia/Alamy: 31c. Daniel E.
Wray/Image Works/Topfoto: 30t. Every effort has been made to trace the copyright holders for the photos used in this
book. The publisher apologizes, in advance, for any unintentional omissions and would be pleased to insert the appropriate
acknowledgements in any subsequent edition of this publication.

Printed in the United States of America

1 2 3 4 5 6 7 8 9 10 09 08 07 06

Words that appear in the glossary are printed in
boldface type the first time they occur in the text.

Contents

This jar is made of glass.

This jar is made of clear glass.

The glass for this jar began as heaps of sand, limestone, and soda ash, with some **recycled** glass added. These materials turn into glass when they are mixed together and heated to a high temperature.

Glass is hard to explain. Some people think it is a liquid because, when glass is hot, it moves around like water. As it cools, however, glass hardens. Most people say glass is a solid because it keeps its shape after it has become hard.

Before a glass factory makes jars, the workers talk to the customer, which is the company that needs jars for its **products**. They discuss what will be put into the jars as well as the jars' shape, size, and color. A designer creates pictures of various jar shapes. The customer can then choose the best shape for the job,

Designers use computers to show customers what the jars they want might look like.

and the factory can begin to make the jars in large quantities.

Why glass?

People have been using glass containers to store food for thousands of years. Glass is a good material to use for food and drink storage because it can be cleaned easily, and it does not rot or rust. Glass can be used to store almost anything. It is often transparent, or clear, so people can see what is inside the jar and how much is left.

Glass jars help keep both wet and dry foods fresh.

Glass is made of sand, limestone, and soda ash.

Sand is the most important **raw material** for making glass. Sand is made of rocks and shells that, over time, have been broken down into tiny grains by weather and water. Big machines dig sand out of the ground. The digging forms huge pits called quarries.

A digger works in a sand quarry.

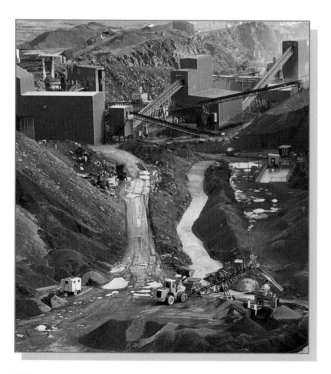

Limestone is another raw material used to make glass. It is rock that formed from dead sea creatures buried in the earth millions of years ago. Machines dig limestone from quarries, too. The sand and limestone may be taken to a glass factory by boat, truck, or train.

A limestone quarry is a huge hole in the ground.

A material called soda ash is also needed to make glass. Most soda ash is made in factories, from salt and other chemicals. Some soda ash forms naturally and can be found in dried-up lakes.

Natron is a type of soda ash that forms as a crust on top of some lakes.

In the Past

Many historians believe that the people who lived where Syria is today, made the first glass about five thousand years ago. No one knows for sure how people discovered glassmaking. It might have been an accident. Maybe someone lit a fire on a sandy sea shore, and limestone and soda ash happened to be in the sand. Tiny drops of glass may have formed at the edge of the fire.

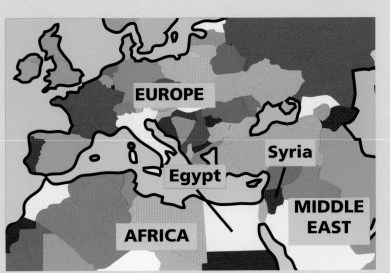

Modern-day Syria is in the Middle East, near Egypt. This is where glassmaking began five thousand years ago.

The materials arrive at the glass factory.

sand

soda ash

limestone

The ingredients used to make glass are sand, limestone, and soda ash.

When the raw materials reach the glass factory, workers unload them and take them into the **batch house**. Glassmakers weigh out the correct amounts of sand, limestone, and soda ash that are needed to make glass. Then, they place the raw materials in a furnace, which is a very hot place that looks like a huge baker's oven. In the furnace, the raw materials melt together to form **molten** glass. The furnace works all day.

Sand alone can be made into glass, but it has to be heated to an incredibly high temperature — about 3,100 °Fahrenheit (1,700 °Celsius). By adding limestone and soda ash to the sand, glass forms at a much lower temperature.

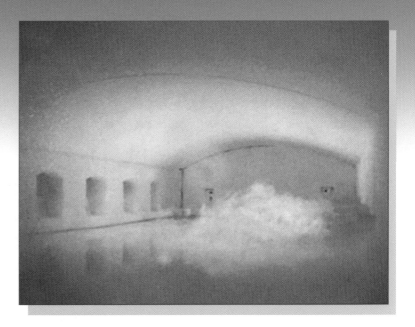

Molten glass forms when a furnace heats a mixture of sand, limestone, and soda ash to about 1,292 °F (700 °C). Water boils at 212 °F (100 °C), so this temperature is very hot.

In the Past

Historians believe that ancient Egyptians made the first glass bottles about 3,500 years ago. The Egyptians formed a bottle shape from sand and dung and then dipped it into molten glass several times. After the shape cooled, it was possible to shake the sand **mold** out of the inside of the bottle. The ancient Egyptians used bottles for perfumes, makeup, precious oils, and medicines.

Ancient Egyptians made bottles like this one for perfume or medicine. They decorated the bottles by adding strands of hot colored glass on the outsides.

Many glass jars are made from recycled glass.

Recycled glass comes from used glass jars and bottles. Many people put their used glass into recycling bins at home, work, school, stores, or restaurants. People can also take used glass to recycling centers.

In some areas, it is important to keep recyclable materials in separate containers.

In many places, trucks collect used glass. They pick it up from schools, homes, and offices and take it to recycling centers.

A worker empties a recycling bin into a collection truck.

All types of glass can be recycled, not just jars.

Used glass is taken to a glass-recycling factory to be cleaned and crushed. A moving belt, called a **conveyor belt**, carries the glass through the factory for processing.

This used green glass is on its way to be recycled.

In the Past

People used to return empty glass bottles to the store where they bought the bottles. Stores paid a small amount of money for each empty bottle. Then the stores sent the bottles back to the original food or drink factories. The factories cleaned, refilled, and sold the bottles back to the stores. This return process still happens in some countries. Returned bottles can be used over and over again.

People and machines clean the pieces of recycled glass.

Any materials that are mixed in with the glass need to be removed. As the broken glass moves through the factory on conveyor belts, it, first, passes under magnets to remove any pieces of metal.

The glass passes under strong magnets inside the white, triangle-shaped parts of the machine. Any magnetic metal sticks to the magnets.

Then, another type of machine uses lasers to find and remove any pieces of ceramic, such as broken cups or plates. Ceramics can damage a glass furnace.

This machine uses lasers to find ceramic pieces.

Next, the broken glass passes workers who pick out any objects that are not glass.

Factory workers wear thick gloves so they will not be cut by the glass.

Why glass?

Glass is a beautiful material to work with. Even everyday glass bottles sparkle when they are clean. Glass can be made in many different colors by adding certain chemicals to glass ingredients. The shine of glass has led artists and craftspeople to use it to make beautiful pictures and designs. These "stained glass" pictures have been used for windows in churches, homes, and many other buildings.

Beautiful patterns and pictures can be created with stained glass.

The pieces of glass are crushed.

A crusher smashes broken glass into even smaller pieces. This finely crushed glass is called **cullet**. A conveyor belt takes the cullet out of the factory, where it is piled up in huge heaps until it is needed.

Conveyor belts move glass out of the factory.

Workers put cullet in heaps for later use.

A clear jar made of recycled glass needs clear glass cullet as well as some new sand, limestone, and soda ash. Trucks bring these materials to the factory the same way they bring materials to make brand new glass. Workers weigh the correct amount of each material and take the ingredients to the furnace room.

Why recycle glass?

1. It takes a lot of heat and energy to make glass from just sand, limestone, and soda ash. Recycled glass does not have to be heated to as high a temperature. Using less energy creates less pollution.

2. The more we use recycled glass, the less we have to dig up the landscape for new raw materials. Digging up the earth uses a lot of energy and destroys the countryside.

3. People who recycle glass keep it separate from the rest of their trash. Unfortunately, large amounts of glass still end up in **landfill sites**, where the glass is lost forever. A landfill site takes up a lot of space, and living near one is not pleasant. Landfills are also costly to run.

A furnace melts all the materials together.

The furnace melts the materials and changes them into molten glass. Molten glass is very hot, and it is runny like syrup or honey. Rivers of glass leave the furnace to go to the part of the factory where they will be turned into jars.

When the glass leaves the furnace, it is very hot.

As the molten glass cools, a machine with huge scissors cuts it into equal-sized pieces, called gobs. The factory workers set up the machine to make the gobs just the right size for a glass jar.

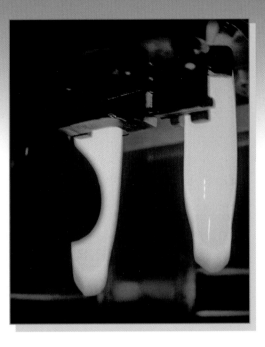

Gobs of hot glass pass along to the next machine.

Why glass?

Once it is in a molten state, glass can be made into many shapes and sizes. Glass is often made into flat sheets for windows. The sheets of glass are called float glass because they are made by floating hot, molten glass on a bath of molten metal, usually tin. The glass spreads out and gradually hardens as it cools. It passes over cooling rollers until it is hard enough to be cut into the correct size for windows.

The raw materials are fed into the float glass furnace.

The materials melt in the furnace.

A machine forms gobs of glass in jar-shaped molds.

Jar-shaped molds are part of the **forming machine**. A piece of the machine seals the top of the mold once the glass gob is inside. Then, from the bottom, a plunger moves up inside the gob, pushing the

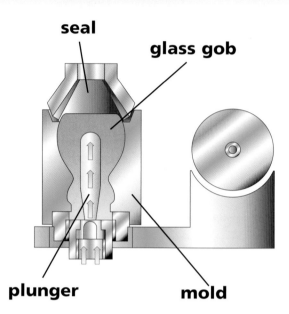

seal

glass gob

plunger

mold

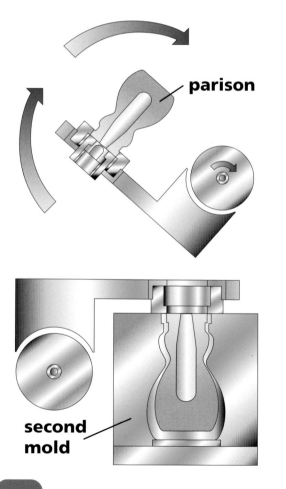

parison

second mold

glass out to the mold's sides. The mold opens to reveal the partly-shaped jar, upside down and still very hot. At this point the jar is called a **parison**. The forming machine now turns the parison upright, onto its base.

A second, slightly bigger, mold closes around the parison.

The glass slowly runs down, until it reaches the bottom of this second mold.

Then the machine blows jets of air into the jar, pushing the hot glass out to the sides of the mold. The glass is then thinner and the jar is bigger.

jets of air

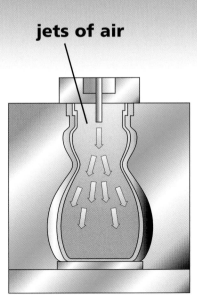

In the Past

Glassblowing is a way of making glass containers by blowing air inside molten glass. People learned how to blow glass in the first century B.C. The glassblower dipped his hollow pipe into molten glass and then slowly turned the pipe around and around. He then rolled the glass gob on an iron slab, blew air down the pipe to expand the gob, and reheated the glass back in the fire so that he could keep working with it. After the glassblower finished the glass object, he cut it off his pipe. He then allowed the glass to cool down.

In this nineteenth-century drawing, French glassblowers are making bottles by blowing air down long pipes.

Hot jars leave the forming machine.

Tongs pick up the hot jars and take them off the forming machine.

Cold air blows around the jar to cool it off. Then the jar is placed on a conveyor belt and travels away from the forming machine.

The surface of each jar is given a coating to make it stronger during its lifetime. Then the jar travels to a large oven called a **lehr**.

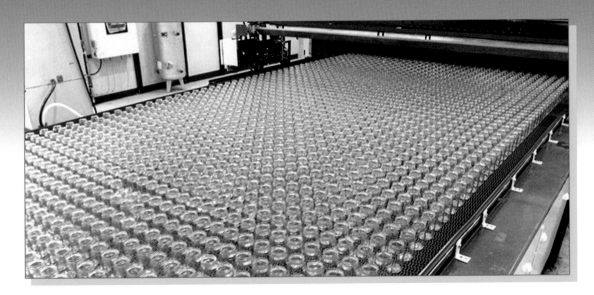

The jars leave the lehr after 20 to 40 minutes.

In the lehr, the jar heats up to 1,022 °F (550 °C), and then it cools down gradually. The lehr removes any cracks or weak points that may have been created during the forming process. As the jar leaves the lehr, the outside is coated again to stop it from getting scratches.

In the Past

For almost two thousand years, glass jars and bottles were made by glassblowers. In 1886, in Britain, Howard Ashley finished the design of a machine that was able to make two hundred glass bottles per hour. He was not able, however, to make his invention successful. Then, in 1903, Michael J. Owens, from Illinois, developed a much faster, fully automatic, bottle-making machine that could make 2,500 glass bottles per hour. His machines were used for decades.

The Owens Bottle Company made a glass bust of Michael J. Owens in 1928.

Every jar is checked to make sure it is perfect.

The jar passes through machines that automatically check for problems. The machines can measure whether the glass of the jar is the correct thickness. The machines can also spot any cracks or other problems. Any jars that are not good enough to be used end up back in the piles of broken glass that are made into cullet and melted down to make into more glass.

The rejected glass piles up until it is ready to be recycled.

If the machines do find problems with the glass, they send information to the operators so that the glass-making machines can be fixed.

Why glass?

Glass can be shaped in many ways. Some bottles and jars have such a special shape that we know instantly what will be inside them. The Coca-Cola company started selling their famous soft drink in specially shaped glass bottles in 1915. Heinz Tomato Ketchup is another bottle shape that many people recognize.

Do you know what is inside these bottles?

d.

a.

b.

c.

Answers:
a. Coca-Cola
b. Orangina
c. Tabasco sauce
d. Perrier mineral water

The jars are ready to leave the factory.

As jars are finished, they are packed into trays. Workers stack up the trays into towers. To stop the jars from knocking against each other and possibly breaking, machines wrap the trays tightly in plastic. The jars are then ready to travel to the customer that asked for them to be made. Many customers send the jars to factories where machines fill them with food such as fruit, coffee, jelly, or olives. A metal or plastic screw-on lid is added to close the jar.

These jars are being filled with coffee.

Another machine sticks a label onto the jar. Now the jar is finally ready to be sold in stores.

When the jar is empty, it can be recycled, and the glass from the jar will be made into a new jar — maybe in a different shape — at the glass recycling factory.

The label tells us what is in the jar.

John Landis Mason with his Mason jars.

In the Past

Hundreds of people have designed glass jars for preserving fruit and vegetables, but John Landis Mason's are the most famous. In 1858, he invented a metal lid that screwed onto his jars to seal the contents quickly and effectively. People continue to use Mason jars in the United States today. The original jars are worth a lot of money.

How a Recycled Glass Jar Is Made

1. Sand, limestone, and soda ash arrive at the glass-recycling factory.

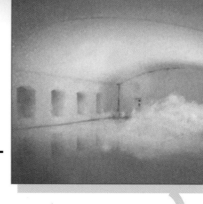

4. Workers measure sand, limestone, soda ash, and crushed glass (cullet) and place them in the furnace.

2. Used glass bottles and jars arrive at the glass-recycling factory.

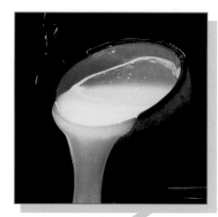

5. Glass forms in the furnace and leaves as rivers of molten glass.

3. The used glass is cleaned to remove any unwanted material.

6. The molten glass is cut into gobs.

9. Jars are checked for cracks or problems. Some jars are rejected and recycled.

10. Jars are filled with food and sent to stores.

8. Hot glass jars are put into the lehr to get rid of cracks and make them strong.

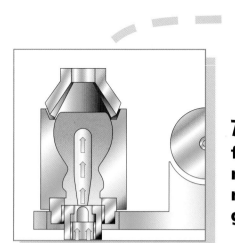

7. The forming machine makes glass jars.

11. A jar is full and ready to be sold.

Other Uses for Glass

Look around you to see how many
different types of glass you can see.

Have you ever used a telescope
or a microscope? Glass lenses are
used in these instruments to bring
distant objects closer to your eyes
or to make small objects look bigger.

Does anyone you know wear glasses?
Special glass can be shaped to make lenses
for glasses so that people can see clearly.

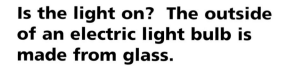

Is the light on? The outside
of an electric light bulb is
made from glass.

Is there a television or computer in the room? Most TV or computer screens are made from a special type of glass that contains lead or barium. The lead and barium absorb harmful X-rays that would otherwise escape from the TV or computer.

Are there any beautiful glass ornaments or glass objects in the room? People sometimes add lead to glass to make it sparkle and shine. Lead also makes glass easier to cut and engrave, which can add to its beauty.

Do you need a drink? Glass is made into open-top containers that we can drink from.

If you are in the kitchen, you may see special types of strong glass that are used for parts of the stove, oven, or microwave. Special, strong glass can also be made into pots and pans that can be heated without breaking.

A mirror is made of glass. It is coated on the back with a thin layer of silver, or another shiny metal, to make it reflect images.

Up in the roof of your home or school, matted strands of glass, called glass wool, help trap heat like a blanket.

People can look through panes of glass in windows and doors of buildings.

When mixed with plastic, glass fibers make a material called fiberglass. It can be mixed with other materials to make helmets and parts of cars and boats, such as the body of this speed boat.

Glass can be made shatter-proof by adding a thin layer of special plastic. The strengthened glass is used to make the windshields of cars, rockets, and tanks. Whole buildings can be covered with strengthened glass.

Glossary

batch house – the area of a glass factory where raw materials are prepared

conveyor belt – a moving belt or long surface used to transport goods or objects around a factory

cullet – the name given to finely broken glass

forming machine – the machine that uses molds to change hot gobs of glass into glass jars or bottles

landfill sites – huge holes in the ground used for burying waste

lehr – a huge oven, or kiln, used to heat glass jars and get rid of cracks

molten – made into a liquid by heating

mold – a container that gives shape to glass and other materials

parison – a partly shaped lump of glass that will become a jar or bottle

products – objects made for certain uses

raw material – something from which a product can be made. The raw materials used to make glass are sand, limestone, and soda ash.

recycled – made from used products such as newspaper or glass jars, and turned back into useful material

Index